Color & Learn Easy
ITALIAN
PHRASES FOR KIDS

Roz Fulcher

ballare
bah-**lahr**-reh

Dover Publications, Inc.
Mineola, New York

This handy book will have you speaking Italian in no time! More than sixty illustrated pages include commonly used words and phrases in both Italian and English. Below each Italian word or phrase you'll find its pronunciation. A syllable that is **boldfaced** should be stressed.

Whether it's just for fun, for travel, or to have a conversation with a friend or relative, you'll find out how to talk about the weather, tell what you'd like at mealtime, and many other helpful phrases—and you can color while you learn!

Copyright

Copyright © 2015 by Dover Publications, Inc.
All rights reserved.

Bibliographical Note

Color & Learn Easy Italian Phrases for Kids is a new work, first published by Dover Publications, Inc., in 2015.

International Standard Book Number

ISBN-13: 978-0-486-80359-3
ISBN-10: 0-486-80359-7

Manufactured in the United States by RR Donnelley
80359702   2016
www.doverpublications.com

Good morning.

Hello.   Good-bye.

See you later.

What's your name?

My name is _____.

Ecco
eh-koh

1. mia madre
mee-ah **mah**-dreh

2. mio padre
mee-oh **pah**-dreh

3. mia sorella
mee-ah soh-**reh**-lah

4. mio fratello
mee-oh frah-**teh**-loh

This is my   1. Mother   2. Father
                3. Sister   4. Brother

How old are you? I am _____ years old.

I'm allergic to nuts/eggs.

I love you.

What's for breakfast?   1. Cereal

2. il toast
eel toast

3. le uova
leh **woh**-vah

2. Toast   3. Eggs

It's time for lunch. I want. . . 1. a sandwich

2. un yogurt
oon **yoh** gert

3. un hamburger
oon **ham**-bur-gur

2. Yogurt   3. Hamburger

I'm hungry! What's for dinner?

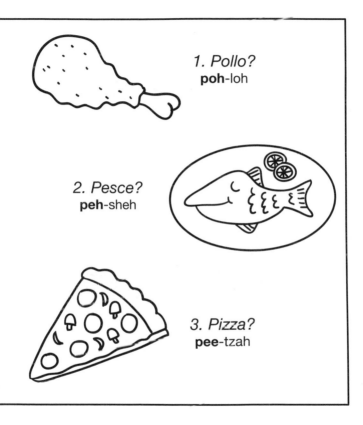

1. Pollo?
poh-loh

2. Pesce?
peh-sheh

3. Pizza?
pee-tzah

1. Chicken?   2. Fish?   3. Pizza?

15

What's for dessert?

1. Gelato?
jeh-**lah**-toh

2. Frutta?
froo-tah

3. Biscotti?
bees-**koh**-tee

1. Ice cream   2. Fruit   3. Cookies

I like to . . .   1. Read   2. Dance

4. *andare in bicicletta*
ahn-**dah**-reh een bee-chee-**cleh**-tah

3. *disegnare*
dee-seh-**nyah**-reh

3. Draw   4. Bike

1. I'm sorry.   2. Don't worry.

3. It's okay.

Can you help me, please? I'm lost.

Buon Natale!

bwon nah-**tah**-leh!

Merry Christmas!

Felice anno nuovo!

ʃeh-**lee**-cheh **ah**-no **nwo**-voh!

Happy New Year!

This is delicious! I'd like some more.

Where are you from?   I am from _____.

I giorni della settimana

eeh **jor**-nee deh-lah set-tee-**mah**-nah

Monday   *lunedì*
loo-neh-**dee**

Tuesday   *martedì*
mahr-teh-**dee**

Wednesday   *mercoledì*
mehr-koh-leh-**dee**

Days of the week

Thursday		*giovedì* joh-veh-**dee**
Friday		*venerdì* veh-nehr-**dee**
Saturday		*sabato* **sah**-bah-toh
Sunday		*domenica* doh-**meh**-nee-kah

I mesi
eeh **meh**-see

January	February	March
gennaio	*febbraio*	*marzo*
jeh-**nah**-yoh	feb-**brah**-yoh	**mahrt**-zoh

April	May	June
aprile	*Maggio*	*giugno*
ah-**pree**-leh	**mah**-djoh	**joon**-yoh

Months

July

luglio
lool-yoh

August

Agosto
ah-**goss**-toh

September

settembre
set-**tem**-breh

October

ottobre
ot-toh-breh

November

novembre
noh-**vem**-breh

December

dicembre
luh dee-**chem**-breh

29

I numeri
eeh noo-**mare**-ee

uno
oo-noh

due
doo-eh

tre
treh

quattro
kwaht-troh

cinque
cheen-kweh

Numbers

sei
say

sette
set-teh

otto
ot-toh

nove
noh-veh

dieci
dee-**eh**-chee

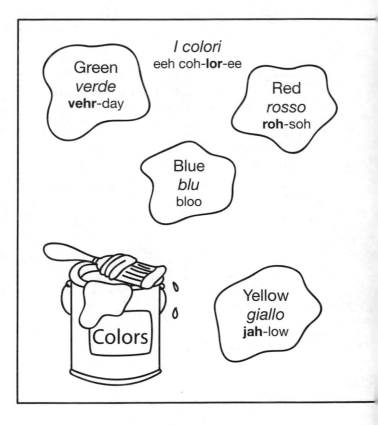

I colori
eeh coh-**lor**-ee

Green
verde
vehr-day

Red
rosso
roh-soh

Blue
blu
bloo

Colors

Yellow
giallo
jah-low

Colors

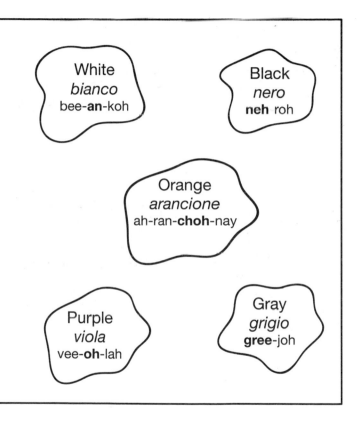

White
bianco
bee-**an**-koh

Black
nero
neh roh

Orange
arancione
ah-ran-**choh**-nay

Purple
viola
vee-**oh**-lah

Gray
grigio
gree-joh

33

1. Let's go to the park!
2. Awesome idea!

1. How much does it cost?
2. It's one dollar.

Let's go to the beach! I will get . . .

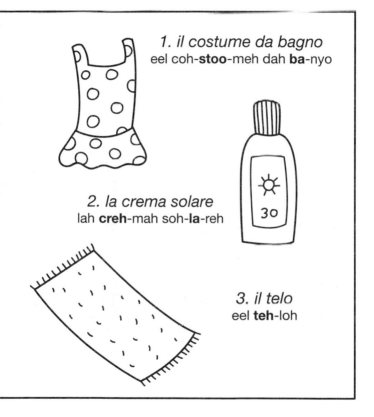

1. *il costume da bagno*
eel coh-**stoo**-meh dah **ba**-nyo

2. *la crema solare*
lah **creh**-mah soh-**la**-reh

3. *il telo*
eel **teh**-loh

1. my bathing suit   2. my lotion   3. my towel

Please.

Thank you.   You're welcome.

It's raining. I'm taking . . .

1. my umbrella   2. my raincoat

Could you speak more slowly?

It's hot today. I'll wear . . .

1. una maglietta
oo-nah mah-lee-**eh**-tah

2. i pantaloncini
eeh pahn-tah-lohn-**chee**-nee

3. i sandal
eeh **sahn**-dah-lee

1. a T-shirt   2. shorts   3. sandals

It's snowing! I need . . .

1. una sciarpa
oo-nah shee-**ahr**-pah

2. i guanti
eeh **gwahn**-tee

3. gli stivali
luh-yee stee-**vah**-lee

4. un cappotto
oon kah-**poh**-toh

1. my scarf   2. my gloves
3. my boots   4. my coat

I'm cold. I need . . .

1. una maglia
oo-nah **mahl**-yah

2. una coperta
oo-nah coh-**per**-tah

3. una giacca
oo-nah **jah**-kah

1. a sweater   2. a blanket   3. a jacket

Do you speak English?

Sorry, I don't understand.

I'm thirsty. I want . . .

1. *l'acqua*
lah-kwah

2. *il succo*
eel **sooh**-koh

3. *il latte*
eel **lah**-teh

1. water   2. juice   3. milk

Excuse me.

1. *Dov'è il ristorante più vicino?*
doh-veh eel ree-stoh-**rahn**-teh pyoo vee-**chee**-noh

2. *Dov'è la fermata dell'autobus più vicina?*
doh-veh lah fair-**mah**-tah dehl-auto-**boos** pyoo vee-**chee**-nah

3. *Dov'è la metropolitana più vicina?*
doh-veh lah meh-tro-po-lee-**tah**-nah pyoo vee-**chee**-nah

Where is the nearest . . .
1. restaurant?   2. bus stop?
3. subway?

53

Do you have a pet?   I have . . .

1. un cane
oon **kah**-neh

2. un gatto
oon **gah**-toh

3. un pesce
oon **peh**-sheh

4. un uccello
oon oo-**cheh**-loh

5. un criceto
oon kree-**cheh**-toh

1. a dog   2. a cat   3. a fish
4. a bird   5. a hamster

Happy birthday! My birthday is in

_____.

Can I . . . 1. Watch TV?
        2. Go to a movie?
        3. Go outside?

Where is the bathroom?

1. *nonna*
noh-nah

2. *nonno*
noh-noh

3. *zia*
tsee-ah

4. *zio*
tsee-oh

5. *cugina*
ku-**jee**-nah

6. *cugino*
ku-**jee**-noh

1. Grandma
2. Grandpa
3. Aunt
4. Uncle
5. Cousin (girl)
6. Cousin (boy)

I don't feel well. My . . . 1. throat   2. head
                        3. stomach . . . (hurts)

I'm tired. Time for bed.

Good night.